JAN   2008

LIVING WELL

SCHOOL SAFETY

by Lucia Raatma

THE CHILD'S WORLD®
CHANHASSEN, MINNESOTA

The Child's World®

Published in the United States of America by The Child's World®
P.O. Box 326, Chanhassen, MN 55317-0326
800-599-READ
www.childsworld.com

Subject Consultant:
Cynthia Klingel,
Mankato Area Public
Schools, Curriculum
Director, Mankato,
Minnesota

Photo Credits: Cover: Image Source/Punchstock; Getty Images/Photodisc: 8 (D. Berry/ Photolink), 9, 13 (Eyewire), 20 (David Toase), 22 (Don Farrall), 25 (Mel Curtis), 26 (Caroline Woodham); Getty Images/Photodisc/SW Productions: 5, 24; Picture Quest: 10 (Mark Andersen/Rubber Ball Productions), 10 right (Image Source/elektraVision), 11 (SWP, Inc./Brand X Pictures), 15 right (Stockbyte), 16 (Corbis), 18 (Thinkstock), 19 (S. Meltzer/Photo Link), 21 (Patrick Sheandell O'Carroll/Photo Alto), 27 (Rubber Ball Productions); Punchstock: 12 (Corbis), 15 (Stockbyte), 17 (Photodisc), 23 (Banana Stock); Richard Cummings/Corbis: 14; SW Productions/Brand X Pictures/Picture Quest: 6, 7.

The Child's World®: Mary Berendes, Publishing Director

Editorial Directions, Inc.: E. Russell Primm, Editorial Director; Elizabeth K. Martin and Katie Marsico, Line Editors; Olivia Nellums, Editorial Assistant; Susan Hindman, Copy Editor; Susan Ashley, Proofreader; Peter Garnham, Fact Checker; Tim Griffin/IndexServ, Indexer; Elizabeth K. Martin and Matthew Messbarger, Photo Researchers and Selectors

Library of Congress Cataloging-in-Publication Data
Raatma, Lucia.
  School safety / by Lucia Raatma.
      p. cm.— (Living well)
Includes index.
Contents: Why is school safety important?—How can you stay safe getting to school?—
How should you act on the playground?—How can you be safe in your school?—What
dangers are at school?—What should you remember about strangers?
  ISBN 1-59296-089-8 (Library Bound : alk. paper)
  1. Schools—Safety measures—Juvenile literature. [1. Schools—Safety measures. 2. Safety.]
I. Title. II. Series: Living well (Child's World (Firm))
  LB2864.5.R33 2004
  363.11'9371—dc21   2003008036

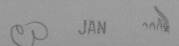

TABLE OF CONTENTS

CHAPTER ONE

4 No Bullies at This School

CHAPTER TWO

6 How Can You Stay Safe Getting to School?

CHAPTER THREE

12 How Should You Act on the Playground?

CHAPTER FOUR

15 How Can You Be Safe in Your School?

CHAPTER FIVE

20 What Dangers Are at School?

CHAPTER SIX

24 What Should You Remember about Strangers?

28 Glossary

28 Questions and Answers about School Safety

29 Helping a Friend Learn about School Safety

29 Did You Know?

30 How to Learn More about School Safety

32 Index

CHAPTER ONE

No Bullies
at This School

Brian tried not to watch as Joe, the playground **bully,** stole a

backpack from Michael, the new kid in his class. Michael had been

sitting by himself. He looked helpless as Joe and his buddies tossed the

backpack back and forth among them. Then Michael got up and

approached Joe. "Please give that back to me," he said in a low voice.

Joe answered him with a shove that knocked him to the ground.

Finally, Brian couldn't take it anymore. "Cut it out," he demanded as

he walked up to the group. He caught the backpack in mid-toss. "And

leave him alone."

Joe looked surprised. "We were just kidding around," he mumbled.

Then a few of Brian's friends joined the crowd. "Well, kid around

someplace else," one of them said. Joe and his buddies backed off and walked away. Brian reached down and helped Michael off the ground.

"Thanks," Michael said quietly.

"No problem," Brian answered. "How about you meet us for lunch in the cafeteria today?"

If you and your friends stick together, you can stop bullies from being unkind to other students.

Michael smiled and nodded. "That would be great," he said.

You spend lots of time at your school, so it is important to keep it safe. You don't have to let bullies take over your school. Help out your friends and stick together. There are other ways you can keep your school safe, too. Following these suggestions can help you make sure your school is a fun and safe place to learn.

CHAPTER TWO

HOW CAN YOU STAY
SAFE GETTING TO SCHOOL?

Many people ride a bus to and from school each day. The bus ride

can be a time to read. Or it can give you a chance to talk to your

friends. No matter how you use this time, staying safe on the bus

is important, too.

Times goes by faster if you wait at the bus stop with your friends!

Be sure to get to your bus stop on time. Try to wait for the bus at a place where others are also waiting. This makes the time before the bus arrives more fun, and it's safer than waiting alone. When the bus arrives, stay at least 10 feet (3 meters) away until

It's important to wait your turn when boarding the bus.

the bus stops. The driver cannot see you if you are too close.

Once the driver opens the doors, wait your turn to get on. Use the handrail as you enter the bus. Try to quickly find a seat, so that the other passengers can board after you. On the bus, the driver is in charge, so you should always listen to his or her instructions. During the bus ride, be sure to stay in your seat. Never put your arms or head

Always be polite to other students as you leave the bus.

out a window. Keep the aisles clear by not placing your backpack or

other belongings there.

Don't stand up until the bus has come to a complete stop. When

you leave the bus, do not push others or be impatient. Be careful that

your clothing and backpack do not get caught on the door or other

parts of the bus. Once you are off, stand clear of the bus. If you have to cross the street, wait until the driver tells you it is safe. Walk

about 10 feet (3 m) in front of the bus, where the driver can see you.

If the bus has started moving, you need to wait. Follow these same

rules when you take the bus home each day.

Other people get to

school in cars, on foot, or by

riding bikes. If you arrive by

car, always wear your seat

belt, and make sure you are

dropped off right in front of

the school. Look for other

cars as you get out. If you are

picked up in a car each day,

wait in a spot where you can

Be sure to buckle up if someone drives you to school in a car.

be easily seen by the driver. Again, look out for other cars as you walk

toward yours. Never get in a car with someone you do not know.

If you walk or bike to and from school, talk to your parents about

the best **route.** Know the houses and stores along your route. Be

aware of people you can trust in case you

need help. Look both ways before

crossing each street. On a bike, always

If you walk to and from school each day, think about asking friends to walk with you.

Riding a bike to school can be fun, but always wear your helmet!

wear a helmet. If you are riding in the street, ride in the same

direction as the cars do. If you can ride on the sidewalk, watch out

for other people. To keep your bike safe, be sure to lock up your bike

while you are at school.

CHAPTER THREE

HOW SHOULD YOU
ACT ON THE PLAYGROUND?

Spending time on the playground is fun. There are many games you can play and great **equipment** you can use. But there are rules to follow to keep the playground a safe place.

While spending time on the playground, never forget the few simple safety rules you have learned.

Pay attention to the clothing you are wearing. Try to avoid wearing sweaters and jackets that have long strings. These can get caught on swings and slides. Keep your shoes on, and make sure they are tied.

Be extra careful when climbing on playground equipment. Make sure the equipment is dry, so you do not

Always stay seated when riding a swing.

slip. You should tell an adult if any of the equipment is broken.

When you are on a swing, always stay seated. Standing might seem like fun, but it can be **dangerous.** Slow down before you get off a swing. You could get hurt if you jump. And don't walk too close to others who are swinging. You might get hit accidentally!

If you decide to play on the slide, it is important to wait your turn. Use the ladder and hold on with both hands. Never climb up the front of a slide. You could get hit by people coming down. And always slide down feet first.

Most kids look forward to time on the playground, but some do not because they are afraid of other kids. Bullies can be mean, and they often use the playground as a place to tease their classmates. If someone is teasing you, tell them to stop. If they don't, just walk away. Stay close to friends you can trust. Tell a teacher or another adult if the bully will not leave you alone.

Don't forget to go down feet first on the slide!

CHAPTER FOUR

HOW CAN YOU BE SAFE
IN YOUR SCHOOL?

You spend a lot of time at school in classrooms. Some simple rules

can make your classroom a safe place. Always sit at your desk. Never

stand on the seat or on top of the desk. Keep

your chair and desk level. Leaning back

and rocking in your chair is dangerous

because your chair could turn over. You

You should always remain seated at your desk (above). Standing on top of your desk (above right) is dangerous and might get you in trouble.

or someone behind you could easily get hurt. Also, keep books and bags out of the aisle so that others will not trip over them.

In the halls of your school, walk but do not run. Running inside the building is not safe for you or for others. Hallways can be slippery. If you turn a corner too quickly, you might bump into another student. It is especially important to be careful and take your time when going up and down stairs. If you trip, you could fall and injure yourself or someone else.

It is also a good idea to keep your locker neat. Too many disorganized items in a locker can be dangerous. They can fall out when

Never run in the hallways at school. You might trip or run into another student.

When you and your friends carry your food trays to your table, use both hands.

you open your locker. Remember to be cautious when opening your

locker door so you don't hit other students with it.

Never climb in or out of windows at your school, except in an

emergency. Always use doors and stairways.

In the cafeteria, be careful when you are carrying a tray of food.

Watch out so you don't bump into other students. And don't try to

balance your tray and an armful of books. If you do have an **acci-**

dent and spill your food, be sure the mess is cleaned up right away.

If there's an emergency at your school, it's important to use the correct exit to leave the building.

This will keep others from falling on a slippery floor.

Your school probably has a fire drill a few times each year. These drills are important. They teach you what to do in case of a fire. Follow the instructions your teachers give you during a drill. Move quickly, but do not run. Go to the correct exit and leave the building. You should take a fire drill seriously so you can be prepared if you are ever really in a fire. If this happens, remember what you learned in the drill. Never hide in a classroom. Wait outside with the other students and the teachers for the firefighters to arrive.

Never go back into the school during a fire.

Fires and other emergencies are not joking matters. Never pull a fire alarm as a joke. These alarms tell firefighters to come to your school. If they answer an alarm that isn't real, they waste time and might be late to help at a real fire.

FIRE ALARM CONTROLS INSIDE

Another Fire Drill?

Does your school have a lot of fire drills? Do you get bored with having to practice so many times? Do you sometimes act silly and not pay attention during a drill? If so, remember that fire drills can help save lives. These drills are exercises to teach you and other students what to do in case of fire. You learn how to leave your school quickly and safely. Without drills, people could easily be frightened or unsure how to escape a building that is on fire.

Your school is not the only place that has fire drills. Many office buildings have them, and so do businesses. Even airports and boats practice fire drills. And every family should practice fire drills at home. The more you know about fire, the better prepared you will be!

CHAPTER FIVE

WHAT DANGERS
ARE AT SCHOOL?

Schools are usually safe places. But like anywhere else, there are

dangers you should be aware of. If you follow a few simple rules

and pay attention to what is going on around you, you can stay

safe and continue learning.

Following some basic rules will help you keep your school a safe place to learn.

Drugs are dangerous to you and other students. They have no place in your school.

If you ever see another student with drugs or alcohol, tell an adult immediately. Cigarettes, drugs, and alcohol do not belong at your school. If another student offers you any of these, say no.

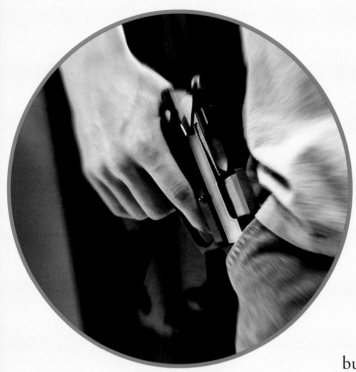

Let a teacher know right away if someone at your school has a gun.

Walk away. Then find an adult and explain what happened. Some students may think that drinking and doing drugs is cool, but it is not. Using cigarettes, drugs, and alcohol can hurt you. Give yourself a chance for a bright future by staying away from them.

School **violence** has been in the news a lot in the last few years. Hearing about problems at other schools might be scary for you. But you can help keep your school a safe one. Never bring guns, knives, or any other **weapons** to school. And if you ever see other kids with these weapons, tell an adult right away. If you hear one student talking about hurting another student, you should never keep it to yourself. It is important to find an adult you trust and tell what you know. In this case, you are not being a tattletale. You are keeping yourself and others safe.

Dangerous Groups

Most of your friends are probably fun. You play together, visit each others' homes, and share secrets. But maybe there are kids who aren't fun to be around. In some places, these groups are called gangs. They are found more often in cities, but small towns can have them, too. Members of gangs have to pass certain illegal tests--like stealing something to get in. These tests might be illegal—like stealing something from a store or even hurting someone. Other tests might be dangerous—like riding a bike too fast. Once in a gang, members might be told to fight with other gangs.

If you are approached by kids from gangs, stay away. Tell them you have your own friends and you don't need to be part of their group. Talk to an adult if you are worried about gangs at your school.

CHAPTER SIX

WHAT SHOULD YOU REMEMBER ABOUT STRANGERS?

Strangers are people you do not know. Pay attention to any strangers you see spending time outside your school or around the playground. If a stranger offers you a ride, say no. Quickly find an adult and explain what happened. If a stranger ever offers you drugs or candy, you should also say no. And again, tell an adult immediately.

A stranger might try all sorts of things to trick you. He might say he lost

Some strangers may try to offer you drugs.
Always say no and tell an adult immediately.

24

If some comes to pick you up, but doesn't know your family code word, don't get in the car.

a kitten and needs your help to find it. He might say your mom sent

him to pick you up.

Talk to your family about having a code word. This is a special

word that your family chooses together. If your parents cannot pick

you up, someone else (possibly a stranger) may have to get you. That person would be told the code word ahead of time. When picking you up, that person would tell you what the word is. That way, you would know whom you can trust. If the stranger does not know the code word, go back in your school and get help. If the stranger tries to touch you, yell as loud as you can. Don't be afraid to make lots of noise.

Talk to your parents about strangers. Be sure you understand who strangers are. Make a list of adults you know and can trust.

During a family meeting, decide upon a code word that everyone will remember.

Yell loudly if a stranger tries to grab you.

There are many adults who care about you. They want to keep you

safe. And many of those adults are right inside your own school.

Glossary

accident (AK-sih-duhnt) An accident is an event that takes place unexpectedly and often involves people being hurt.

bully (BUL-ee) A bully is a person who frightens or picks on others.

dangerous (DAYN-jur-uhss) Something that is dangerous is not safe and is likely to cause harm.

emergency (i-MUR-juhn-see) An emergency is a sudden and dangerous situation. It requires immediate attention.

equipment (i-KWIP-muhnt) Equipment is a collection of machines or tools for a given purpose. Playground equipment includes slides, swings, tunnels, bars, and other items.

route (ROOT) A route is a path or course that you follow from one place to another.

violence (VYE-uh-luhnss) Violence is the use of physical force. People are violent when they destroy things or hurt people.

weapons (WEP-uhnz) Weapons are items that can be used in a fight or attack.

Questions and Answers about School Safety

What if I want to hang out with the cool kids, but the cool kids do drugs? If kids are doing drugs, they are not cool. They are probably angry or sad about something. Spend more time with friends who aren't involved in drugs. Talk to an adult about what to do.

My best friend is constantly teasing a new student who is shy. What should I do? Tell your friend to knock it off! Remind him what it is like to be the new kid. Encourage him to get to know your new classmate instead. Suggest things you and your friend can do with the new student.

What if a stranger pulls up at the bus stop and says my mom asked her to pick me up? Ask for the family code word. If the stranger doesn't know it, walk away immediately and tell a teacher or another adult.

I overheard a classmate say he has a gun and he can "take care" of the playground bully. He is just kidding, right? He might not be. Talk to a teacher or another adult right away.

Helping a Friend Learn about School Safety

▸ You and a friend can look out for each other. Let your friend know that she can depend on you if someone at school is bullying her.

▸ Talk to your friend about the rules for staying safe on the bus. Wait for the bus where the driver can see you. And remind your friend to make sure his clothing and backpack do not catch on the door as he gets on or off the bus.

▸ Talk to your friend about guns and other weapons at school. Agree that you will both tell an adult if you ever see other students with weapons or hear other students talk about bringing weapons to school.

▸ Work with your friend to find safe games to play during recess. Steer clear of the kids who play rough.

Did You Know?

▸ Bullies make up a small group in most schools, but they cause lots of problems. If all the other students told the bullies to stop, wouldn't the bullies be surprised!

▸ You might be afraid to talk to some of your teachers—they might seem scary! But they are there to help you, and they want to listen if there are problems. They want to help keep you safe.

▸ Some kids dread eating in the cafeteria each day. They might be uncomfortable around the other students. You can help by inviting them to eat lunch with you.

How to Learn More about School Safety

At the Library: Nonfiction
Chaiet, Donna, and Francine Russell. *The Safe Zone.*
New York: Morrow Junior Books, 1998.

Gutman, Bill. *Harmful to Your Health.*
New York: Twenty-First Century Books, 1996.

Sanders, Pete, and Steve Myers. *Personal Safety.*
Brookfield, Conn.: Copper Beech Books, 1999.

Schwartz, Linda. *What Would You Do? A Kid's Guide to Tricky and Sticky Situations.*
Santa Barbara, Calif.: Learning Works, 1990.

Silverstein, Alvin, Virginia Silverstein, and Laura Silverstein Nunn. *Staying Safe.*
New York: Franklin Watts, 2000.

At the Library: Fiction
Fitts, Stuart. *A Stranger in the Park.* Salt Lake City, Utah: Agreka Books, 1999.

McCain, Becky Ray. *Nobody Knew What to Do.*
Morton Grove, Ill.: Albert Whitman & Company, 2001.

Naylor, Phyllis Reynolds. *The King of the Playground.* New York: Atheneum, 1991.

Rathmann, Peggy. *Officer Buckle and Gloria.* New York: Putnam, 1995.

On the Web
Visit our home page for lots of links about school safety:
http://www.childsworld.com/links.html

Note to Parents, Teachers, and Librarians: We routinely verify our
Web links to make sure they're safe, active sites—so encourage your
readers to check them out!

Through the Mail or by Phone

American Red Cross National Headquarters
431 18th Street, N.W.
Washington, DC 20006
202/303-4498

National Center for Injury Prevention and Control
4770 Buford Highway, N.E.
Atlanta, GA 30341
770/488-1506

National SAFE KIDS Campaign
1301 Pennsylvania Avenue, N.W.
Suite 100
Washington, DC 20004
202/662-0600

National Safety Council
1121 Spring Lake Drive
Itasca, IL 60143
630/285-1121

National School Safety Center
141 Duesenberg Drive
Suite 11
Westlake Village, CA 91362
805/373-9977

The Nemours Center for Children's Health Media
Alfred I. duPont Hospital for Children
1600 Rockland Road
Wilmington, DE 19803
302/651-4046

Index

alcohol, 21–22

bicycles, 10–11
bullies, 4–5, 14
bus drivers, 7, 9
buses, 6–9

cafeteria, 17
chairs, 15
cigarettes, 21–22
classrooms, 15–16
clothing, 12
code words, 25–26

desks, 15
doors, 17
drugs, 21–22, 24

emergencies, 17, 19

fire alarms, 19
fire drills, 18, 19
fires, 18–19

gangs, 23

guns, 22–23

hallways, 16
helmets, 11

knives, 22–23

lockers, 16–17

playgrounds, 12–14, 24

rules, 15

seat belts, 9
slides, 14
spills, 17–18
stairways, 16, 17
strangers, 24–26
swings, 13

violence, 22

walking, 9, 10
weapons, 22–23
windows, 17

About the Author

Lucia Raatma received her bachelor's degree in English literature from the University of South Carolina and her master's degree in cinema studies from New York University. She has written a wide range of books for young people. When she is not researching or writing, she enjoys going to movies, practicing yoga, and spending time with her husband, their daughter, and their golden retriever. She lives in New York.